FIRST THINGS TO HAND

ALSO BY ROBERT PINSKY

POETRY

Jersey Rain
The Figured Wheel
The Want Bone
History of My Heart
An Explanation of America
Sadness and Happiness
The Inferno of Dante (translation)

PROSE

The Life of David
Democracy, Culture and the Voice of Poetry
The Sounds of Poetry
Poetry and the World
The Situation of Poetry
Landor's Poetry

ANTHOLOGIES

An Invitation to Poetry
Americans' Favorite Poems
Poems to Read
Handbook of Heartbreak

FIRST THINGS TO HAND

ROBERT PINSKY

QUARTERNOTE CHAPBOOK SERIES #5
SARABANDE BOOKS
LOUISVILLE, KENTUCKY

No part of this book may be reproduced without written permission of the publisher. Please direct inquiries to:

Managing Editor
Sarabande Books, Inc.
2234 Dundee Road, Suite 200
Louisville, KY 40205

Library of Congress Cataloging-in-Publication Data

Pinsky, Robert.
  First things to hand : poems / by Robert Pinsky.— 1st ed.
      p.   cm. — (Quarternote chapbook series ; #5)
  Includes bibliographical references and index.
  ISBN 1-932511-34-2 (pbk. : acid-free paper)
  I. Title. II. Series.
  PS3566.I54F57 2006
  811'.54—dc22   2005022249

13-digit ISBN 978-1-932-51134-5

Cover image: *Raja Sidh Sen of Mandi as a Manifestation of Shiva,* Indian, Pahari, about 1725. Provided courtesy of the Museum of Fine Arts, Boston. Photograph © 2006 Museum of Fine Arts, Boston.

Cover and text design by Charles Casey Martin

Manufactured in Canada
This book is printed on acid-free paper.

Sarabande Books is a nonprofit literary organization.

THE KENTUCKY ARTS COUNCIL

The Kentucky Arts Council, a state agency in the Commerce Cabinet, provides operational support funding for Sarabande Books with state tax dollars and federal funding from the National Endowment for the Arts, which believes that a great nation deserves great art.

CONTENTS

First Things to Hand

1. First Things to Hand

In the skull kept on the desk.
In the spider-pod in the dust.

Or nowhere. In milkmaids, in loaves,
Or nowhere. And if Socrates leaves

His house in the morning,
When he returns in the evening

He will find Socrates waiting
On the doorstep. Buddha the stick

You use to clear the path,
And Buddha the dog-doo you flick

Away with it, nowhere or in each
Several thing you touch:

The dollar bill, the button
That works the television.

Even in the joke, the three
Words American men say

After making love. *Where's*
The remote? In the tears

In things, proximate, intimate.
In the wired stem with root

And leaf nowhere of this lamp:
Brass base, aura of illumination,

Enlightenment, shade of grief.
Odor of the lamp, brazen.

The mind waiting in the mind
As in the first thing to hand.

2. Book

Its leaves flutter, they thrive or wither, its outspread
Signatures like wings open to form the gutter.

The pages riffling brush my fingertips with their edges:
Whispering, erotic touch this hand knows from ages back.

What progress we have made, they are burning my books, not
Me, as once they would have done, said Freud in 1933.

A little later, the laugh was on him, on the Jews,
On his sisters. O people of the book, wanderers, *anderes*.

When we have wandered all our ways, said Ralegh, Time
Shuts up the story of our days—beheaded, his life like a book.

The sound *bk:* lips then palate, outward plosive to interior stop.
Bk, bch: the beech tree, pale wood incised with Germanic runes.

Enchanted wood. Glyphs and characters between boards.
The reader's dread of finishing a book, that loss of a world,

And also the reader's dread of beginning a book, becoming
Hostage to a new world, to some spirit or spirits unknown.

Look! What thy mind cannot contain you can commit
To these waste blanks. The jacket ripped, the spine cracked,

Still it arouses me, torn crippled god like Loki the schemer
As the book of Lancelot aroused Paolo and Francesca

Who cling together even in Hell, O passionate, so we read.
Love that turns or torments or comforts me, love of the need

Of love, need for need, columns of characters that sting
Sometimes deeper than any music or movie or picture,

Deeper sometimes even than a body touching another.
And the passion to make a book—passion of the writer

Smelling glue and ink, sensuous. The writer's dread of making
Another tombstone, my marker orderly in its place in the stacks.

Or to infiltrate and inhabit another soul, as a splinter of spirit
Pressed between pages like a wildflower, odorless, brittle.

3. Glass

Waterlike, with a little water
Still visible swirled in the bottom:

Earth changed by fire,
Shaped by breath or pressure.

Seemingly solid, a liquid
Sagging over centuries
As in the rippled panes
Of old buildings, Time's
Viscid pawprint.

Nearly invisible.
Tumbler. Distorting,
Breakable—the splinters
Can draw blood.

Craft of the glazier.
Ancestral totem substance:
My one grandfather
Washing store windows
With squeegee and bucket,
The other serving amber
Whiskey and clear gin over the counter,

His son my father
An optician, beveling lenses
On a stone wheel. The water
Dripping to cool the wheel
Fell milky in a pale
Sludge under the bench
Into a galvanized bucket
It was my job to empty,
Sloshing the ponderous
Blank mud into the toilet.

Obsidian, uncrystallized silicate.

Unstainable or stained.
Mirror glass, hour glass, dust:
Delicate, durable measure.

4. Jar of Pens

Sometimes the sight of them
Huddled in their cylindrical formation
Repels me: humble, erect,
Mute and expectant in their
Rinsed-out honey crock: my quiver
Of detached stingers. (Or, a bouquet
Of lies and intentions unspent.)

Pilots, drones, workers. The Queen is
Cross. Upright lodge
Of the toilworthy, gathered
At attention as though they believe
All the ink in the world could
Cover the first syllable
Of one heart's confusion.

This fat fountain pen wishes
In its elastic heart
That I were the farm boy
Whose illiterate father
Rescued it out of the privy
After it fell from the boy's pants:
The man digging in boots
By lanternlight, down in the pit.

Another pen strains to call back
The characters of the thousand
World languages dead since 1900,
Curlicues, fiddleheads, brushstroke
Splashes and arabesques:
Footprints of extinct species.

The father hosed down his boots
And leaving them in the barn
With his pants and shirt
Came into the kitchen,
Holding the little retrieved
Symbol of symbol-making.

O brood of line-scratchers, plastic
Scabbards of the soul, you have
Outlived the sword—talons and
Wingfeathers for the hand.

5. Photograph

Light-inscribed
Likeness

Vulnerable to light,
To the oils of the hand.

The paper sensitive
The dyes ephemeral

The very medium
A trace of absences.

Speed of the years
Speed of the shutter.

The child's father
Crouches level to her

With the camera and so
She crouches too.

Agile the dancer.
Little room

Of the camera, wide
Gaze of exposure—

Shiva the maker
Shiva the destroyer:

The flash of your hammer
Fashions the shelter.

6. Other Hand

The lesser twin,
The one whose accomplishments
And privileges are unshowy: getting to touch
The tattoo on my right shoulder.
Wearing the mitt.

I feel its familiar weight and textures
As the adroit one rests against it for a moment.
They twine fingers.

Lefty continues to experience considerable
Difficulty expressing himself clearly
And correctly in writing.

Comparison with his brother prevents him
From putting forth his best effort.

Yet this halt one too has felt a breast, thigh,
Clasped an ankle or most intimate
Of all, the fingers of a hand.

And possibly his trembling touch,
As less merely adept and confident,
Is subtly the more welcome of the two.

In the Elysian Fields, where every defect
Will be compensated and the last
Will be first, this one will lead skillfully
While the other will assist.

And as my shadow stalks that underworld
The right hand too will rejoice—released
From its long burden of expectation:
The yoke of dexterity finally laid to rest.

7. Door

The cat cries for me from the other side.
It is beyond her to work this device
That I open and cross and close
With such ease when I mean to work,

Its four panels form a cross—the rood,
Impaling gatepost of redemption.
The rod, a dividing pike or pale
Mounted and hinged to swing between

One way or place and another, meow.
Between the January vulva of birth
And the January of death's door
There are so many to negotiate,

Closed or flung open or ajar, valves
Of attention. O kitty, If the doors
Of perception were cleansed
All things would appear as they are,

Infinite. Come in, darling, drowse
Comfortably near my feet, I will click
The barrier closed again behind you, O
Sister will, fellow mortal, here we are.

21

Pliers

What is the origin of this despair I feel
When I feel
I've lost my grip, can't manage a thing?

Thing
That means a clutch of contending voices—
So my voice:

When my mongrel palate, tongue, teeth, breath
Breathe
Out the noise *thing* I become host and guest

Of ghosts:
Angles, Picts, Romans, Celts, Norsemen,
Normans,

Pincers of English the conquered embrace.
Embrace
Of the woman who strangled her sister one night,

All night
Moaning with the body held in her arms.
The arms

Of the pliers I squeeze hard squeeze its jaws
And my jaw
Clenches unwilled: brain helplessly implicated

In plaited
Filaments of muscle and nerve. In the enveloping
Grip of its evolution

Chambered in the skull, it cannot tell the tool
From the toiler
Primate who plies it. Purposeless despair

Spirits
The ape to its grapples, restless to devise.
In the vise-

Grip *Discontent*, the grasper's bent.

Banknote

Behind city walls, calm rituals of exile.
The Brazilian cleaner hums and sponges the table.
A civil quiet between us I will not break

By chanting my gratitude in broken Polish.
She has the courage to be my great-grandfather Ike.
Thanks to his passage a century ahead of hers

I get to sit at the table, I write the check.
To recite this to him through her would be foolish.
Her only language for now is Portuguese,

Though every week she knows more English words.
On the Brazilian equivalent of a dollar bill,
Not only a portrait of Drummond de Andrade

But an entire poem by him: nineteen lines.
It makes the dollar look—Philistine. The poem
Is about a poem he intends to write about

The single diamond made of all our lives.
From gluts, dearths. From markets, forced migrations.
Nossas vidas formam um só diamante.

Sicilian Archimedes could move this adamant
Prism that we form, if he could stand outside it.
Locked blind in the diamond, its billion cuts and facets,

Molecules in an obdurate equilibrium
Of pressures, we cannot see the shifting fire.
Words on the banknote; the banknote tints the words.

From Ruth the Moabite, her great-grandson David.
And from Ruth's sister Orpha, Goliath the gentile.
Signature graffiti sprayed on security shutters

In characters the corrugations disable:
In the unpeace, the breaking of the wards?
The pyramid eye envisions networks of cable,

Gulfs arched, wilderness paved. In the system
Of privilege and deprivation, the employed, the avid:
Fraught in the works, turning the gear of custom.

Newspaper

They make the paper with an invisible grain,
So you can tear straight down a vertical column.
But if you try to tear it crosswise, it rips
Out of control in jagged scallops and slashes.
Here amid columns is a man who handles
Search dogs. He says the dogs depend on rewards.
But not like the dogs I know, not dog treats: the Lab
Who'll balance one on his muzzle, trembling and gazing
Up at you till you say *"okay"* then he whips
The thing up into the air and snaps it and bolts it.
No, what the handler says is that his dogs
Are trained to find survivors—that's their reward,
Finding somebody alive is what they want.
And when they try and try and never get it,
They get depressed, he says: *These dogs are depressed.*
Yes, what an animal thing depression is,
The craving for some redemption is like a thirst.
It's in us as we open the morning paper:
Fresh, fallible, plausible. It says the smoke
Is mostly not flesh or paper. First white, the drywall,
Then darker pulverized steel and granite and marble,
And then, long-smouldering toxic plastic and fiber.
How toxic, they don't know or it doesn't say.

In the old days, the printing plant and "the paper"
(Meaning the Globe or Herald or Journal or Times)
Were in one building, and the tremendous rolls
Of newsprint tumbled off the trucks each day.
When I was small one crushed a newsboy's legs.
There was a fund for him, I remember his picture
Accepting a powered wheelchair, in the paper—
Paper, the bread of Chronos, titanic Time
That eats its children: the one-way grain of downward
Irrevocable channels, the crosswise jumble,
Darkness innate in things. In the weather. In the boy
Who beams up at the camera or down at his stumps.
In the prisoner who speaks an unknown language
So that his captors guess and call him "the Chechen."
The errant, granular pulp. In some old stories,
The servant rises early and reads the paper,
Then gets the iron and presses it flat and smooth
To place by the master's breakfast—the skin of days.

NOTE

Thing, thyngan: *verb.*

From Old English *thyngian,* to parley, to assemble, to confer, to make terms or come to terms, determine, discourse, address. Compare Old Norse *thynga:* to hold a public meeting or to confer. Also, Old High German *dingôn:* to hold a court, to conduct a lawsuit, to negotiate a compromise or terms of peace.

Thing: *noun.*

Forms: **þing, þinge, thyng, thinge, thynge.** [Old English *þing;* Old Frisian. *thing, ting*]: assembly, council, lawsuit, matter. Old Saxon *thing:* an assembly for judicial or deliberative purposes, conference, transaction, matter, object.

Old High German *ding, dinc:* a public assembly for judgment and decision, law-court. Danish *ting:* a court of justice. Norwegian *ting* (neuter): a public assembly; also a creature, a being.

That which is stated or thought; an opinion; a notion; an idea.

A suit, a plaint, a decision, a discourse or a giving voice. A convocation or parliament of voices. The *thingstead* is the place of discussion or parley.

From a discussion, or assembly or law court comes the sense of a matter at hand, an issue for debate. And from that sense comes eventually the nearly opposite sense of a concrete object.

THE AUTHOR

ROBERT PINSKY was born in Long Branch, New Jersey, and attended Rutgers and Stanford, where he held a Stegner Fellowship in Creative Writing. He has taught classes in poetry at Wellesley, Berkeley, and currently at Boston University.

Among his awards are the William Carlos Williams Prize, the Shelley Memorial Award, and the Lenore Marshall Poetry Prize. His translation *The Inferno of Dante* was awarded the *Los Angeles Times* Book Award. From 1997 to 2000 he was the U.S. Poet Laureate.

His books include *The Want Bone, The Figured Wheel: Collected Poems 1966–1996,* and *Jersey Rain.* His Tanner Lectures at Princeton University were published as *Democracy, Culture, and the Voice of Poetry.*

COLOPHON

Set in Hiroshiga
with Zapf Humanist.
Designed and typeset by
Charles Casey Martin.
Printed by Friesens, Canada.